W9-BSV-276

The
Aldus Guide to
Basic Design

by Roger C. Parker

The Aldus Guide to Basic Design was written under the auspices of Aldus Corporation, developers of PageMaker® desktop publishing software, Seattle, Washington.

This booklet was illustrated and produced by Laura Lewis Graphic Design. It was created with PageMaker 1.2 and the Linotronic™ 100P imagesetter.

COPYRIGHT
© 1987 by Aldus Corporation. All rights reserved. No part of this publication may be reproduced, transmitted, transcribed, stored in a retrieval system, or translated into any language in any form by any means without the written permission of Aldus Corporation.

ISBN 0-941719-00-6
Printed in USA

Table
of Contents

57 Part Four: Apply the Finishing Touches

63 Part Five: Review the Four Steps to Success

65 Conclusion

INTRODUCTION

The purpose of graphic design is to make it as easy as possible for readers to understand your message. Graphic design is a tool, not an end in itself. Graphic design should be unobtrusive. It succeeds to the extent it becomes transparent. Success is measured by how quickly and effectively you communicate your ideas to the reader.

Our purpose in writing this booklet is to help you produce better-looking, easier-to-read publications — regardless of whether they're advertisements, annual reports, books, brochures, newsletters, training manuals, or personnel forms. We want to make it easy for you to make the most of the power built into the latest desktop publishing software programs.

Desktop publishing software programs permit you to manipulate type and graphic images on the screen of your computer. In minutes, you can do what it would take previous generations of designers hours, even days, to do, using traditional typesetting, layout, and paste-up techniques.

By eliminating the expensive, time-consuming aspects of page design, desktop publishing software programs expand your creative abilities. Because you spend less time on production, you can spend more time designing for clarity and impact.

Part One:
Basic Concepts

Graphic design presents you with tremendous challenges and opportunities. This is partly because there are no universal rules for graphic design. But there are guidelines that can be adapted to most situations. Together, they provide a framework for your design approach, ensuring that your publication receives the kind of attention it needs to transmit its message effectively.

EXPERIMENTATION

Be willing to experiment.

Although many feel graphic design is based on intuitive flashes of brilliance, design excellence is usually the result of trial and error.

Professional graphic designers rarely solve design problems on their first try. Rather, most designers spend hours sketching out solutions that might work. Each sketch builds on the strengths of the previous sketch, eliminating the weak elements.

Desktop publishing software programs permit you to follow this same procedure — even if you can't draw a straight line. On the screen of your computer, you can experiment with various arrangements of type and artwork.

When you have arrived at a visual solution or page layout that works, print it out and save it.

Then, continue working on it. When you have finished your revisions, print it out again. If it's better than the original version, save it. But, if it isn't as good as your first attempt, return to your original file.

Without investing great amounts of money or time, you can easily try out various design solutions until you come up with the best one possible.

APPROPRIATENESS

Be flexible in applying the rules that follow.

There are no hard and fast rules for graphic design. Advice that works in one circumstance will not necessarily work in another. Success in graphic communications is based on appropriately relating the elements of graphic design to their surroundings. Choose the particular arrangement that works best in its particular environment.

Appropriateness is based on proportion. The size of any graphic element should be based on the size of the page, the graphic elements that surround it, and the emphasis you want it to receive.

Appropriateness also relates to the publication's audience and content. Whether or not a graphic solution is appropriate depends on two issues: how much it furthers the publication's purpose and whether it is suitable for your audience. A legal document for the United States Supreme Court should have a totally different appearance than a supermarket handout.

CONSISTENCY

Be consistent.

Be consistent in the way you handle the various elements of graphic design. Be consistent both within each page and within a publication.

If you use 1-inch margins on page 1, for example, use 1-inch margins throughout the publication. If some of your headlines are set flush left, all headlines should be set flush left. Do not change typeface or type size unless there are compelling reasons to do so — such as when you want to attract attention.

Inconsistent handling of design elements leads to confusion. Confusion will weaken your publication.

STYLE

Do not try to create a design style.

Style is a natural, subtle outgrowth of your particular way of achieving consistency and appropriateness. Style reflects the particular solutions you use to solve the design problems you encounter as you produce publications. Style is not created. It evolves naturally out of practice and experience.

Your graphic design efforts will begin to exhibit a style as you become successful in using the tools of graphic design to communicate your ideas as simply and effectively as possible.

BALANCE

Avoid static balance.

Balance can lead to boredom and interrupted eye movement. Indecision and interrupted eye movement occur when the reader's eyes are faced with equal-sized elements.

Tension adds interest to a page. Unequal left/right or top/bottom balance helps provide movement. Tension can be created by using white space around type or artwork.

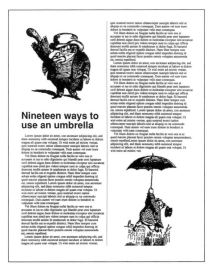

The top and bottom of this page are perfectly balanced. The page lacks visual interest.

A more pleasing page shows two different size graphics. The graphic on the right has been enlarged for visual emphasis, and the copy in the right two columns wraps around the contours of the graphic for additional interest.

UNITY

Organize each page around a single dominant visual element.

A dominant visual unifies the page by providing a focal point and resting spot for the reader's eyes before they begin their travel through the page. A dominant visual avoids the clutter and confusion that occurs when the reader's eyes are presented with an unorganized series of equal-sized graphic elements.

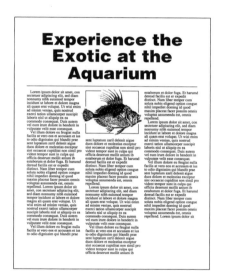

The dominant element can be a headline. . .

a large photograph or illustration. . .

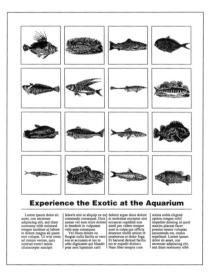

a repeating series of smaller photographs or illustrations. . .

or a large block of copy.

SPREADS

Design your publication in terms of facing pages.

Readers usually view two pages at a time. By concentrating your design efforts on two-page spreads, you avoid creating pages that fight each other when placed side by side.

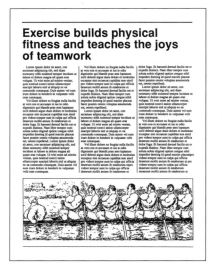

This page looks good on its own.

This page also looks good on its own. . .

Exercise builds physical fitness and teaches the joys of teamwork

(Lorem ipsum placeholder text)

At first you may be stiff and sore, but soon you'll be looking forward to your workouts as you feel better and make new friends

(Lorem ipsum placeholder text)

but together, they are difficult to read. Because the pages are so balanced, there is no starting point and destination for eye movement. The reader finds it difficult to know where to begin reading. As a result, the reader is likely to move on without reading much on the page.

Exercise builds physical fitness and teaches the joys of teamwork

At first you may be stiff and sore, but you'll be looking forward to your workouts as you feel better and make new friends.

(Lorem ipsum placeholder text)

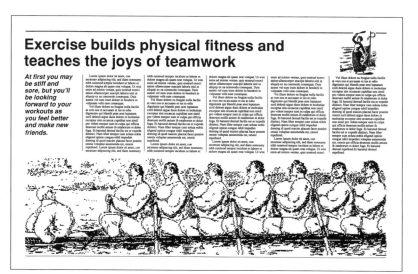

This problem can be handled by working with the two pages as a single unit.

Part Two:
Establish a
Format

Design for readability and uniqueness. Your goal is to make it as easy as possible for readers to understand the points you're trying to make.

Format your publication for easy transitions from section to section. Never allow your reader to get lost. Anything that interrupts smooth eye travel discourages readers from continuing.

The format you establish will set your publication apart from other publications. It will also help you organize your material and add emphasis to important elements. Emphasis can only occur when words and ideas are contrasted against a continuing structure.

GRID

Start by creating a grid.

The grid is one of the most important formatting tools at your disposal. A grid consists of a series of nonprinting horizontal and vertical lines. These define the placement of the graphic elements that make up a printed page. Although these lines do not appear in the printed version, their impact can be felt in a publication's overall organization and consistency.

Grids provide a consistent way of handling diversity. Grids make it possible to maintain page-to-page and issue-to-issue consistency, even though the contents of each page and each issue are constantly changing.

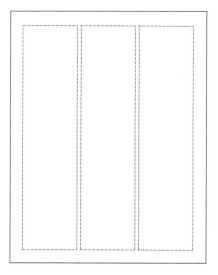

One of the most useful formats is a three-column grid. The three-column grid provides an orderly arrangement of parts, while permitting a surprising degree of flexibility.

Here, for example, headlines, artwork, and body remain anchored to the three-column format.
For variety, an important photograph and story can extend across two columns.

Four- and five-column grids can be used for more complex applications.

MARGINS

Standardize your margins.

Always indent copy, headlines, chapter titles, and page numbers the same distance from the top, bottom, and sides of a page throughout your publication.

Margins isolate your publication from surrounding distractions. Margins provide the space necessary to highlight important information.

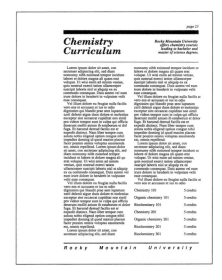

A deep top margin makes it easy to locate and read headlines, chapter titles, and page numbers.

Wide inside margins are appropriate if you are printing on both sides of each page. They allow room for binding. Wide inside margins should also be used if you are going to three-hole–punch your work.

BORDERS

Use borders for visual identity.

Sometimes it is good to frame your pages with strong
borders. Borders are lines that help create and strengthen
the visual identity of your publication.

The same border can be used on all four sides of a page.
This technique creates a dignified or scholarly
appearance.

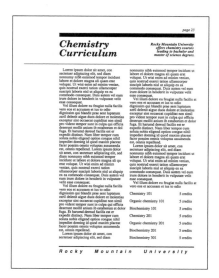

Different borders can be used on the top and sides of a page.

Sometimes, different borders are used to define the top and bottom boundaries of a page.

In this case, the edges of the type and artwork create the vertical borders that define the sides of each page.

Borders do not have to extend the full width of a page to be effective. When they don't, the page takes on an informal or contemporary appearance.

COLUMNS

Organize your body copy into columns.

Choose a column width appropriate to the size of type you are using. Each column of a three-column format should contain approximately 50 characters.

The buzzword for law-office relocation in 1988 is equity. Owning your digs means controlling your economic and spacial destiny, while avoiding the costly chore of moving when business takes off. The value of such an arrangement is clear — it is estimated that construction costs for law-firm space can easily reach $70 a square foot. Finding a building with the right location and space requirements, however, often proves to be an insurmountable obstacle. Affordable buildings with room for expansion usually include loft or warehouse real estate outside the hub of the city — less than ideal accommodations for a growing firm. But fortunately, certain building trends in the '80s have worked to the advantage of professional industries such as legal services. The most important of these is the almost non-stop high-rise

Use wide columns for large type sizes.

The buzzword for law-office relocation in 1988 is equity. Owning your digs means controlling your economic and spacial destiny, while avoiding the costly chore of moving when business takes off. The value of such an arrangement is clear — it is estimated that construction costs for law-firm space can easily reach $70 a square foot. Finding a building with the right location and space requirements, however, often proves to be an insurmountable obstacle. Affordable buildings with room for expansion usually include loft or ware -house real estate out- side the hub of the city — less than ideal accommodations for a grow- ing firm. But fortunately, certain building trends in the '80s have worked to the advantage of professional industries such as legal services. The most important of these is the almost non-stop high-rise office construction that has created a square-foot glut and left many developers shaking in their boots. The builder's dilemma is a tenant's delight — often taking the form of rent abatements, construction packages, and, yes, partial ownership.

An equity position for a law firm translates into tax write-offs, depreciation allowances, additional cash flow, and fixed rent for the life of the lease. Other fiscal bonuses include profits from the eventual sale or refinancing of the asset. The buzzword for law-office relocation in 1988 is equity. Owning your digs means controlling your economic and spacial destiny, while avoiding the costly chore of moving when business takes off. The value of such an arrangement is clear — it is estimated that construction costs for law-firm space can easily reach $70 a square foot. Finding a building with the right location and space requirements, how-

Use narrow columns for small type sizes.

Columns do not have to be the same width. Headlines, subheads, illustrations, and captions can be organized in narrow columns that introduce and support the body copy contained in adjoining wider columns.

The buzzword for law-office relocation in 1988 is equity. Owning your digs means controlling your economic and spacial destiny, while avoiding the costly chore of moving when business takes off. The value of such an arrangement is clear — it is estimated that construction costs for law-firm space can easily reach $70 a square foot. Finding a building with the right location and space requirements, however, often proves to be an insurmountable obstacle. Affordable buildings with room for expansion usually include loft or warehouse real estate outside the hub of the city — less than ideal accommodations for a growing firm. But fortunately, certain building trends in the '80s have worked to the advantage of professional industries such as legal services. The most important of these is the almost non-stop high-rise

Use justified (flush left/flush right) columns to add formality and save space. Justified columns are characterized by lines of identical length. The first and last letters of each line are lined up with the first and last letters of the lines above and below it. Equal line length is achieved by hyphenation and by slightly increasing or reducing word spacing.

The buzzword for law-office relocation in 1988 is equity. Owning your digs means controlling your economic and spacial destiny, while avoiding the costly chore of moving when business takes off. The value of such an arrangement is clear — it is estimated that construction costs for law-firm space can easily reach $70 a square foot.

Finding a building with the right location and space requirements, however, often proves to be an insurmountable obstacle. Affordable buildings with room for expansion usually include loft or warehouse real estate outside the hub of the city — less than ideal accommodations for a growing firm. But fortunately, certain building trends in the '80s have worked to the advantage of professional industries such as legal services.

The most important of these is the almost non-stop high-rise office construction that has created a square-foot glut and left many developers shaking in their boots. The builder's dilemma is a tenant's delight — often taking the form of rent abatements, construction packages, and, yes, partial ownership.

An equity position for a law firm translates into tax write-offs, depreciation allowances, additional cash flow, and fixed rent for the life of the lease. Other fiscal bonuses include profits from the eventual sale or refinancing of the asset. All these benefits result in thousands of extra dollars for law firms that

Use unjustified (flush left/ragged right) columns to create an informal, easy-to-read publication. Unjustified columns are characterized by irregular line endings at the right margin. Words are separated by equal amounts of space. Few words are hyphenated.

RULES

Visually organize your page with horizontal or vertical lines, called rules.

Rules can be thick or thin, depending on how they relate to the copy and white space on each page.

Use vertical rules to separate columns.

Use horizontal rules to separate topics within a column.

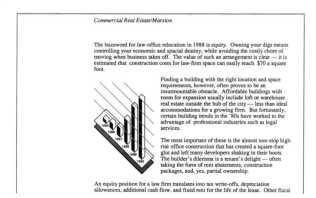

Use either single or double lines. Sometimes, both are used together.

HEADERS AND FOOTERS

Always keep your reader informed.

Information in the top and bottom margins of each page helps readers locate specific information and monitor their progress through your publication.

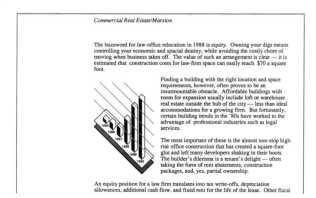

Headers (also called running heads) refer to information contained at the top of each page. Sometimes this information simply repeats the publication's title and the name of the author or firm publishing it. Often, headers identify the chapter or division title.

Equity

The buzzword for law-office relocation in 1988 is equity. Owning your digs means controlling your economic and spacial destiny, while avoiding the costly chore of moving when business takes off.

The value of such an arrangement is clear — it is estimated that construction costs for law-firm space can easily reach $70 a square foot. Finding a building with the right location and space requirements, however, often proves to be an insurmountable obstacle. Affordable buildings with room for expansion usually include loft or warehouse real estate outside the hub of the city — less than ideal accommodations for a growing firm. But fortunately, certain building trends in the '80s have worked to the advantage of professional industries such as legal services.

Square-foot Glut

The most important of these is the almost non-stop high-rise office construction that has created a square-foot glut and left many developers shaking in their boots. The builder's dilemma is a tenant's delight — often taking the form of rent abatements, construction packages, and, yes, partial ownership.

An equity position for a law firm translates into tax write-offs, depreciation allowances, additional cash flow, and fixed rent for the life of the lease. Other fiscal bonuses include profits from the eventual sale or refinancing of the asset.

COMMERCIAL REAL ESTATE • Page 42

Page numbers can be placed at the top of a page or in the information contained in the bottom margins of each page. Information and page numbers located at the bottom of a page are called footers (or running feet).

TYPE

Use type to create a personality for your publication.

Each typeface speaks in a different tone of voice. Type adds personality and expressiveness to your publication. The typefaces you select for headlines, subheads, body copy, and captions affect the way readers experience your ideas.

THE ELEGANT GOURMET

Some typefaces are formal. . .

The Elegant Gourmet

others are informal.

The Elegant Gourmet

Some typefaces are playful. . .

The Elegant Gourmet

others are serious.

Avoid typefaces that draw attention to themselves. These diminish the importance of the message you're communicating.

Type greatly influences the appearance of your publication. Different typefaces have different weights. Thick, or bold, typefaces used in small areas add to the contrast, balance, and tension of the page. Thinner typefaces open up the page, giving the elements more room to breathe.

There are two categories of type, serif and sans serif.

serif type

Serif type is characterized by tiny cross-lines (or feet) at the ends of the main letter strokes. Serif type is ideal for body copy, as the cross-lines contribute an easy letter-to-letter transition for the reader's eyes.

sans serif type

Sans serif type, which is more simple and straight-forward, is ideal for headlines and subheads.

Do not mix too many typefaces on a page or in a publication. Confusion, instead of variety, rapidly sets in. Be consistent throughout your publication in the typefaces you use for headlines, subheads, body copy, and captions.

MASTHEAD AND LOGO

Provide a strong masthead for your publication.

The masthead is your publication's title set in type in a unique way. The masthead is usually the dominant visual element on the first page of a publication. It is a standing element that sets your publication apart from others and provides both visual identification and issue-to-issue consistency.

Masthead and headlines must be sized to work with each other. Neither should dominate the other. Headlines and mastheads perform different functions. The masthead identifies the publication and gives it stability from issue to issue. The headline invites readers to pay attention to the particular topic being discussed.

This masthead overwhelms the headline, making the headline hard to read.

This headline overwhelms the masthead, weakening the publication's visual identity.

This masthead is in a more pleasing proportion to the headlines.

The same rules apply to your firm's logo. "Logo" refers to the unique way your firm's name has been set in type. The size and placement of your logo should also remain consistent from publication to publication.

HEADLINES

Use strong, descriptive headlines to organize your material.

Headlines are among the most important design tools available to you. Headlines help determine the overall appearance of your publication, as well as strengthening the message you want to communicate. Design your headlines so they will transmit the focus of each page to the reader.

Headlines must be large enough for easy reading. Yet, the headlines must not compete with other elements on a page.

The type used in this headline is too large. It overpowers the surrounding area.

This can be corrected by using a smaller type size.

The type used in this headline is too small. As a result, the headline is dwarfed by its surroundings.

Headlines can be:

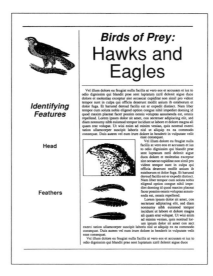

centered. . .

flush left. . .

or flush right. The correct approach depends on how the headline relates to the other visual elements on the page, such as photographs and copy.

Use both uppercase (capital letters) and lowercase type in your headlines. This makes them easier to read.

Reserve the use of uppercase-only headlines to headlines containing just a few words of large type.

CITY ART COLLECTIVE PLANS FESTIVAL

Compare the headline above. . .

City Art Collective Plans Festival

with this one.

SUBHEADS

Place subheads so they provide a transition from headline to body copy.

Subheads expand upon headlines and lead readers into the body copy. Subheads can also guide readers through long blocks of copy. Subheads make it easy for readers to locate information relevant to their needs.

Make subheads stand out from body copy by setting them in boldface type. . .

large type. . .

or placing them next to the body copy they describe.

White space, rules, and other graphic devices can be used in conjunction with subheads to strengthen their impact and create a distinct appearance for your publication.

Use subheads only when an important new topic is introduced. Too many subheads compete with each other and create a cluttered publication.

CAPTIONS

Use captions to describe how photographs and artwork support the body copy.

Captions should be short and to the point.
Captions should be set in small type, so they do not compete with the body copy.

Captions are widely read, giving you an opportunity to summarize important points made in the body copy.

Captions should be set in the same typeface, size, and style throughout a publication. Captions can be placed below, above, or next to a photograph or an illustration.

Captions can be set flush-right to the left border of a photograph or illustration.

Or, you can set captions flush-left to the right border.

Captions can also line up with the top border of a photograph. . .

or the bottom border.

Captions can also be centered. . .

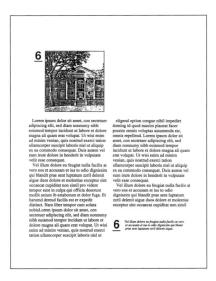

or placed elsewhere on the page and connected to the
artwork with letters or numbers.

COLOR

**Use color to set your
publication apart from others.**

Use colored ink to highlight borders, rules, or headlines.
Or, print your publication on colored paper.

You can also use color as an organizing element.
Different colors can be used to compartmentalize your
publication or draw attention to certain sections.

Choose colors that reflect the message you are
communicating. Bright colors indicate excitement;
subdued colors add dignity.

Remember that less is more. Color gains impact
when used it is used selectively. It loses impact when it
is overused.

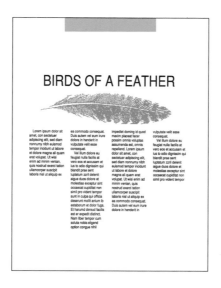

Part Three:
Add Emphasis
Where Needed

Use the tools of graphic emphasis to strengthen the communicating power of your publication. Design emphasis ensures that important ideas attract more attention than supporting arguments, examples, and facts.

TYPE SIZE

Use large type to emphasize important ideas.

Type size should reflect the importance of the various parts of your publication. Headlines should be larger than subheads. Subheads should be larger than body copy. Body copy should be larger than captions and footnotes.

TYPE STYLE

Vary type styles to emphasize important ideas.

Add emphasis to important ideas by setting headlines, subheads, and body copy in variations of the typefaces normally used.

This is boldface type.

Boldface type is authoritative.

This is italic type.

Italic type adds emphasis in a less authoritative way. It provides a refined or elegant mood, or irony and humor.

This is bold-italic type.

Bold-italic type gives a sense of action.

WHITE SPACE

Use white space to make design elements stand out.

White space provides a background that emphasizes whatever it surrounds.

Frame your pages with white space. This strengthens your message by focusing the reader's attention on your words and ideas.

Avoid white space in the middle of a page. This creates unsightly holes, which lead to an unfinished look.

Add emphasis to headlines by surrounding them with white space. White space separates headlines from surrounding body copy and artwork, making the headlines easier to read.

The above headline is difficult to read. Because the type is so large, there's no room for white space. As a result, the headline is too close to the body copy.

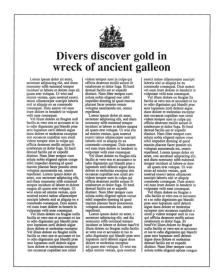

One way of providing more breathing room for your headlines is to set them in a smaller type size. This increases the white space around them, which helps isolate them from surrounding elements.

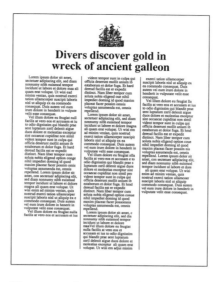

Use unequal amounts of white space to frame the bottoms of columns that are too short to fill the page.

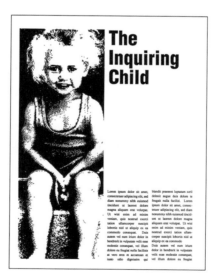

White space can also be used to balance large photographs and blocks of copy.

REVERSES

Use reverse type to call out elements of the page.

Use reverse type (white letters against a black background) to add emphasis to headlines and short blocks of copy.

New annex increases hospital services

Avoid the use of small type in reversed areas. Small type is hard to read when reversed.

New annex increases hospital services

Large reverse type is easier to read.

New annex increases hospital services

Use reverse serif typefaces with discretion.

New annex increases hospital services

Straightforward, sans serif typefaces are easier to read when reversed.

Always use adequate letter spacing and line spacing when type is reversed. Otherwise, it will be difficult for readers to read your words.

SCREENS

Use screens (shades of gray) to attract attention.

Screens can also be used to add interest to pages without photographs or illustrations.

The buzzword for law-office relocation in 1988 is equity. Owning your digs means controlling your economic and spacial destiny, while avoiding the costly chore of moving when business takes off. The value of such an arrangement is clear — it is estimated that construction costs for law-firm space can easily reach $70 a square foot.

You can use dark type against a light screen. . .

The buzzword for law-office relocation in 1988 is equity. Owning your digs means controlling your economic and spacial destiny, while avoiding the costly chore of moving when business takes off. The value of such an arrangement is clear — it is estimated that construction costs for law-firm space can easily reach

or reverse type out of a dark screen.

Consolidated Sales (millions)

Actual   Projected

19				
18				
17				
16				
15				
14				
Q1	Q2	Q3	Q4	Q1

Use screens to highlight photographs, illustrations, graphs, or charts.

Screens can also be used to differentiate sidebars from body copy. Sidebars are short articles or statements that support a major point contained in the body copy.

BOXES

Use boxes to draw attention to elements that would otherwise be dwarfed by their surroundings.

Buying your first home

Lorem ipsum body text (placeholder).

Home Finance Tips:

- Lorem ipsum dolor sit amet, con sectetuer adipiscing elit, sed diam nonummy nibh
- Euismod tempor incidunt at labore et dolore magna ali quam erat volupat
- Ut wisi enim ad minim veniam, quis nostrud exerci tation ullamcorper suscipit
- Laboris nisl ut aliquip ex ea commodo consequat.

Type can be boxed. . .

Buying your first home

Buying a first home may be traumatic for some couples.

and so can photographs and illustrations.

Buying your first home

Boxes can be reversed. . .

Buying your first home

or screened for additional impact.

Buying your first home

Lorem ipsum dolor sit amet, con sectetuer adipiscing elit, sed diam nonnummy nibh euismod tempor incidunt ut labore et dolore magna ali quam erat volupat. Ut wisi enim ad minim veniam, quis nostrud exerci tation ullamcorper suscipit laboris nisl at aliquip ex ea commodo consequat. Duis autem vel eum iriure dolore in hendrerit in vulputate velit esse consequat.

Vel illum dolore eu feugiat nulla facilis at vero eos et accumsan et iusto odio dignissim qui blandit prae sent luptatum zzril delenit aigue duos dore ero molestias excepteur sint occaecat cupiditat non simil pro vident tempor sunt in culpa qui officia deserunt mollit anium ib estaborum et dolor fuga. Et harumd dereud facilis est er expedit distinct. Nam liber tempor cum soluta nobis eligend option congue nihil impedit doming id quod maxim placit facer possim omnis voluptas assumda est, omnis repellend. Lorem ipsum dolor sit amet, con sectetuer adipiscing elit, sed diam nonnummy nibh euismod tempor incidunt ut labore et dolore magna ali quam erat volupat. Ut wisi enim ad minim veniam, quis nostrud exerci tation ullamcorper suscipit laboris nisl at aliquip ex ea commodo consequat. Duis autem vel eum iriure dolore in hendrerit in vulputate velit esse consequat.

Vel illum dolore eu feugiat nulla facilis at vero eos et accumsan et iusto odio dignissim qui blandit prae sent luptatum zzril delenit aigue duos dore ero molestias excepteur sint occaecat cupiditat non simil pro vident tempor sunt in culpa qui officia deserunt molit anium ib estaborum et dolor fuga. Et harumd dereud facilis est er expedit distinct. Nam liber tempor cum soluta nobis eligend option congue nihil impedit doming id quod maxim placit facer possim omnis voluptas assume est, omnis repellend. Lorem ipsum dolor sit amet, con sectetuer adipiscing elit, sed diam nonnummy nibh euismod tempor incidunt ut labore et dolore magna ali quam erat volupat. Ut wisi enim ad minim veniam, quis nostrud exerci tation ullamcorper suscipit laboris ni urt aliquip ex ea commodo consent. Duis autem vel eum iriure dolore in

anium ib estaborum et dolor fuga. Et harumd dereud facilis est er expedit distinct. Nam liber tempor cum soluta nobis eligend option congue nihil impedit doming id quod maxim placit facer possim omnis voluptas assumea est, omnis repellend.

Home Finance Tips:

■ Lorem ipsum dolor sit amet, con sectetuer adipiscing elit, diam nonnumy nibh

■ Euismod tempor incidunt ut labore et dolore magna ali erat volupat

■ Ut wisi enim ad minim ven, quis nostrud exerci tation ullamcorper suscipit

Lorem ipsum dolor sit amet, con sectetuer adipiscing elit, sed diam nonnumy nibh euismod tempor incidunt ut labore et dolore magna ali quam erat volupat. Ut wisi enim ad minim veniam, quis nostrud exerci tation ullamcorper suscipit laboris ni urt aliquip ex ea commodo consequat. Duis autem vel eum iriure dolore in hendrerit in vulputate velit esse consequat.

Vel illum dolore eu feugiat nulla facilis at vero eos et accumsan et iusto odio dignissim qui blandit prae sent luptatum zzril delenit aigue duos dore ero molestias excepteur sint occaecat cupiditat non simil pro vident tempor sunt in culpa qui officia deserunt molit anium ib estaborum et dolor fuga. Et harumd dereud facilis est er expedit distinct. Nam liber tempor cum soluta nobis eligend option congue nihilit impedit doming id quod maxim placit facer possim omnis voluptas assume est, omnis repellend. Lorem ipsum dolor sit amet, con sectetuer adipiscing elit, sed diam nonnummy nibh euismod tempor incidunt ut labore et dolore magna ali quam erat volupat. Ut wisi enim ad minim veniam, quis nostrud exerci tation ullamcorper suscipit laboris nil at aliquip ex ea commodo consequat. Duis autem vel eum iriure dolore in hendrerit in vulputate velit esse consequat. Lorem ipsum dolor sit amet adici odio dignisitm qui blandit prae sent luptatum zzril delenit aigue duos dom

inciduns ut labore et dolore magna ali quam erat volupat. Ut wisi enim ad minim veniam, quis nostrud exerci tation ullamcorper suscipit laboris nil at aliquip ex ea commodo consequat. Duis autem vel eum iriure dolore in hendrerit in vulputate velit esse consequat.

Vel illum dolore eu feugiat nulla facilis at vero eos et accumsan et iusto odio dignissim qui blandit prae sent luptatum zzril delenit aigue duos dore ero molestias excepteur sint occaecat cupiditat non simil pro vident tempor sunt in culpa qui officia deserunt mott anium ib estaborum et dolor fuga. Et harumd dereud facilis est er expedit distinct. Nam liber tempor cum soluta nobis eligend option congue nihil consequat.

Vel illum dolore eu feugiat nulla facilis at vero eos et accumsan et iusto odio dignissim qui blandit prae sent luptatum zzril delenit aigue duos dore ero molestias excepteur sint occaecat cupiditat non simil pro vident tempor sunt in culpa qui officia deserunt mol anium ib estaborum et dolor fuga. Et harumd dereud facilis est er expedit distinct. Nam liber tempor cum soluta nobis eligend option congue nihil impedit doming id quod maxim placit facer possim omnis voluptas assumda est, omnis repellend. Lorem ipsum dolor sit amet, con sectetuer adipiscing elit, sed diam nonnummy nibh euismod tempor incidunt ut labore et dolore magna ali quam erat volupat. Ut wisi enim ad minim veniam, quis nostrud exerci tation ullamcorper suscipit laboris nil at aliquip ex ea commodo consequat. Duis autem vel eum iriure dolore in hendrerit in vulputate velit esse consequat.

Vel illum dolore eu feugiat nulla facilis at vero eos et accumsan et iu

Drop shadows with screens or reverses can be used to draw attention to boxes.

ARTWORK

Highlight your ideas with graphics.

Use photographs, illustrations, charts, and graphs to communicate important ideas at a glance, as well as to add visual variety to your publication.

In addition to emphasizing important points, photographs and illustrations personalize your publication.

Crop photographs so that emphasis is placed on the most important elements.

Here, background details obscure the subject.

When unnecessary details are eliminated, the subject emerges with added impact.

Illustrations also echo the voice of a publication. When used appropriately, they add to the publication's personality.

Illustrations can be as literal or as abstract as desired. They can be used as the dominant visual element on a page or as a background for headlines and body copy.

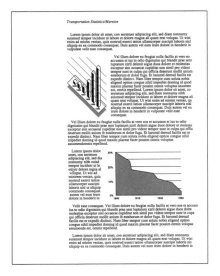

Charts and graphs bring numbers to life. Charts and graphs are especially useful when comparing data.

PULL QUOTES

Strengthen important ideas with pull quotes.

Pull quotes are short quotations used as a graphic device, especially when no artwork is available. Pull quotes summarize surrounding material and draw attention to it.

Pull quotes can be set in large type. . .

Music in America

> *"Her mastery of the art was nothing short of astounding. The audience remained spellbound throughout the performance."*

reversed. . .

Music in America

> *"Her mastery of the art was nothing short of astounding. The audience remained spellbound throughout the performance."*

or boxed.

Part Four: Add The Finishing Touches

Attention to detail can mean the difference between a high-quality publication and a mediocre one.

A little extra effort can help you avoid embarrassing and expensive mistakes. Last-minute revisions can reward you with a publication that is a pleasure to read instead of a struggle.

Here are six ways to make sure you communicate as strongly as possible.

PROOFREADING

Check for text and layout mistakes.

Always check your work before you send it to the printer for duplication.

Make certain that nothing important has been left out. Make sure that names, addresses, and phone numbers are correct.

Ask someone who was not involved in producing your publication to review it. It is very easy to overlook your own mistakes. Your mind unconsciously supplies missing words and corrects misspelled words that would be immediately obvious to others.

Check for graphic consistency as well as accuracy. Pay particular attention to the graphic tools you have used for formatting and emphasis. Make sure that column rules are drawn in, that the bottoms of columns are parallel, and that you have told readers where articles continue on to.

LEADING

To refine the appearance of your publication or adapt text to available space, adjust the vertical spacing between lines of type. This is called leading (pronounced "ledding").

Bold, elegant lines
mark spring fashions

Proper leading ensures that the bottoms of letters in one line do not touch the tops of letters in the next line.

Bold, elegant lines

mark spring fashions

The above headline has too much vertical spacing. The lines do not relate well to each other, making them difficult to read.

Bold, elegant lines
mark spring fashions

Tightening up the leading conserves space and improves both the appearance and readability of this headline.

When adjusting leading, make certain that you do not inadvertently draw attention to one part of your publication at the expense of another. Make sure you do not destroy your publication's graphic consistency. The leading you use for each element of text should be the same throughout your publication.

WIDOWS AND ORPHANS

Avoid short lines of type at the tops or bottoms of columns.

The buzzword for law-office relocation in 1988 is equity. Owning your digs means controlling your economic and spacial destiny, while avoiding the costly chore of moving when business takes off.

The value of such an arrangement is clear — it is estimated that construction costs for law-firm space can easily reach $70 a square foot.

Finding a building with the right location and space requirements, however, often proves to be an insurmountable obstacle. Affordable buildings with room for expansion usually include loft or warehouse real estate outside the hub of the city — less than ideal accommodations for a growing firm. But fortunately, certain building trends in the '80s have worked to the advantage of professional indus-

A widow is a single word or very short line of copy that falls at the end of a paragraph, especially at the bottom of a column.

The buzzword for law-office relocation in 1988 is equity. Owning your digs means controlling your economic and spacial destiny, while avoiding the costly chore of moving when business takes off. The value of such an arrangement is clear — it is estimated that construction costs for law-firm space can easily reach $70 a square foot. Finding a building with the right location, however, often proves to be an

obstacle.

Affordable buildings with room for expansion usually include loft or warehouse real estate outside the hub of the city — less than ideal accommodations for a growing firm. But fortunately, certain building trends in the '80s have worked to the advantage of professional industries such as legal services. The most important of these is the

An orphan is a single word or very short line carried to the top of a column to end a paragraph.

The most common way to eliminate widows and orphans is to edit the copy. By adding a few words to the end of the paragraph in a column of type, you can usually fill out the last line and eliminate the problem.

KERNING

Adjust letter spacing with kerning.

You can improve the appearance and readability of headlines by increasing or decreasing letter spacing. This is called kerning.

Yard Tools

Kerning eliminates the unnaturally large spaces that often occur between certain letter pairs, such as an uppercase T or Y next to a lowercase a, i, or o.

Yard Tools

Kerning brings these letters together, creating a more unified appearance.

Bold lines mark spring fashions

B o l d   l i n e s   m a r k   s p r i n g   f a s h i o n s

You can also kern to expand a headline without increasing its height. This reduces the emphasis of the headline by making it appear lighter in weight.

HYPHENATION

Adjust word spacing with hyphens.

Hyphenate words to correct unnaturally large spaces that occur within, or at the ends of, lines — especially in narrow columns.

Hyphenation is the process of splitting long words into shorter syllables. Often, hyphenating a few words in a paragraph improves the appearance of the entire paragraph.

---

often proves to be an insurmountable obstacle. Affordable buildings with adequate room for expansion usually include loft or warehouse real estate outside the hub of the city — less than ideal accommodations for a growing firm. But fortunately, certain building trends in the '80s have worked to the advantage of professional industries such as legal services. The most

---

Before. . .

---

often proves to be an insur-mountable obstacle. Afford-able buildings with adequate room for expansion usually include loft or warehouse real estate outside the hub of the city — less than ideal accom-modations for a growing firm. But fortunately, certain build-ing trends in the '80s have worked to the advantage of professional industries such as legal services. The most im-portant of these is the almost

---

after.

PUNCTUATION

Pay particular attention to punctuation.

Punctuation is one touch that distinguishes fully designed publications from typewritten or word-processed documents. These differences stand out particularly with apostrophes, quotations, and dashes.

'single quotes' and "double quotes"

Documents prepared on a typewriter or word processor are typically characterized by vertical, rather than curved, quotation marks and apostrophes.

'single quotes' and "double quotes"

Well-designed typeset publications, however, use curved open and close quotation marks and apostrophes.

Use an em dash — instead of two hyphens.

Instead of two hyphens to signal a dash, published documents usually use a single long stroke, called an em dash.

Part Five:
Review the Four
Steps to Success

Designing a publication is similar to assembling a jigsaw puzzle. In each case, your goal is to organize a variety of separate elements.

If you dump a jigsaw puzzle on the table and impatiently begin to work, you're likely to become frustrated by the mass of indistinguishable pieces. But, if you first separate the pieces by color and shape, you'll be able to see what you have to work with. You'll have the preliminary organization necessary to begin assembling your puzzle.

Likewise, you can strengthen your graphic design capabilities by first organizing your project and then proceeding on a step-by-step basis. The following steps review the procedures for producing good-looking, high-impact publications.

Step 1: Plan your project.

Start by gathering together all the materials for your publication. This includes copy, illustrations, and photographs.

Your initial inventory will help you determine how many articles, illustrations, and photographs you'll have to include. Then you can estimate the length and placement of the articles and artwork. At this point, you may find it useful to sketch a reduced-size layout of your publication, called a thumbnail. The thumbnail sketch will help you see whether there's adequate space for all the pieces in your inventory.

Now, define the goals of your project. Ask yourself questions like:

- ■ What is the purpose of the publication?

- ■ Who is the audience?

- ■ What are the important points you want to communicate?

- ■ Which design approach will best attract your audience's attention and communicate your message?

Step 2: Establish a format.

Next, decide on a format. Remember, the format provides page-to-page and issue-to-issue consistency. The format serves as a background for your words and ideas, a structure for all the elements of your publication.

Pay particular attention to the context of your publication. Make certain your project conforms to your firm's established graphic identity. Make sure your publication does not resemble your competitors' efforts.

The format should include some flexibility. White space at the bottoms of columns and between articles, for example, makes it easy to fine-tune your publication at the last minute without destroying page-to-page consistency.

Step 3: Add emphasis where needed.

Successful graphic design makes it easy for readers to separate the important elements from the less important. This is achieved by selectively adding emphasis.

Like the boy who cried "Wolf!" too often, the tools of graphic emphasis lose their impact when they are overused. A cannon exploding in battle is not as dramatic as a candy wrapper rustling during a quiet moment at a symphony concert.

Step 4: Check and re-check your work.

Check your work for accuracy before you take it to a commercial printer for the production of multiple copies.

Pay special attention to names, addresses, and phone numbers. Make certain that you have complied with legal requirements, such as copyright and trademark notices. Then, apply the finishing touches that strengthen the visual presentation of your ideas and make them easier to read. Often, simple changes in word and letter spacing or line endings can improve the appearance and readability of your publication.

Many otherwise successful projects have been torpedoed at the last minute by tiny details that escaped notice until it was too late to correct them.

CONCLUSION

View the development of strong graphic design skills as a process rather than an event.

Search for perfection on a step-by-step basis. Be willing to learn from your mistakes and from the experience of others.

Each time you complete a project, take the time to evaluate it critically. View each completed project not as an end in itself, but as a stepping stone toward better projects in the future. Search for ways to improve your performance the next time around. As you evaluate each project, ask yourself questions like:

- How consistently did I handle the basic design elements?

- Were my design solutions appropriate for each situation?

- Could I have strengthened the formatting of this publication?

- Did I overuse the tools of emphasis?

- Was the artwork effective?

- Did I overlook any last-minute improvements?

By viewing each project as a learning experience, you'll find your graphics skills increasing by leaps and bounds.

In addition, search for inspiration in books and magazines. Read and study how others have solved the same problems you're struggling with.

Analyze the work of others. Try to identify what separates strong publications from weak publications. Keep a scrapbook of ideas that appeal to you. Let the work of others excite and motivate you.

Bibliography

The Chicago Manual of Style: The 13th Edition of a Manual of Style Revised and Expanded, The University of Chicago Press, 1982.
The most comprehensive guide to style available. Especially recommended for preparing book-length publications.

The Copy-to-Press Handbook: Preparing Words And Art For Print, by Judy E. Pickens. John Wiley & Sons, 1985. Filled with practical tips.

Create the Perfect Sales Piece: A Do-It-Yourself Guide to Producing Brochures, Catalogues, Fliers, and Pamphlets, by Robert Bly. John Wiley & Sons, 1986.
Provides a framework for planning your publication and keeping it focused on its intended purpose.

Editing by Design: A Guide to Effective Word-And-Picture Communication for Editors and Designers, by Jan V. White. R.R. Bowker, Company, 1982.
Contains excellent examples of grids and other design elements.

Newsletter Publishing, by Howard Penn Hudson. Charles Scribner's Sons, 1982. Contains many examples of newsletter formats.

Publication Design, 3rd ed., by Roy Paul Nelson. William C. Brown Company, 1984. Contains extremely detailed chapters devoted to newsletters, newspapers, books, and catalogs.

Words Into Type, 3rd ed., by Marjorie E. Skillin, Robert M. Gay, and others. Prentice-Hall, Inc., 1974.
Another comprehensive guide to publication design and text editing.

Aldus Corporation and PageMaker

Graphic designers have used the concepts described on these pages for hundreds of years. In the past, however, the process took a lot of time and cost a lot of money.

In 1985, Aldus Corporation, in Seattle, Washington, introduced PageMaker desktop publishing software to eliminate the tedious, expensive process involved in designing and producing top-quality printed materials. Developed by the publication professionals who founded Aldus, PageMaker turns your personal computer into a sophisticated publishing system.

PageMaker page composition software gives you the help you need to design, lay out, and produce good-looking, high-impact publications, integrating text and graphics from other software programs.

PageMaker replaces the costs and delays of conventional cut-and-paste layout with instantaneous feedback. It permits you to see how your publication will look, instantly, whenever you:

- add or subtract type

- change the typeface, type style, type size, kerning, or leading

- add borders, rules, screens, and reverses

- adjust the number and width of columns

- insert, remove, crop, or resize drawings, charts, and graphs.

PageMaker makes it easy to create a grid with as many elements as necessary to format your publication. PageMaker helps you see at a glance how the parts of your publication fit together as a whole. You can print thumbnail copies of your publication and work on two-page spreads at the same time.

In short, PageMaker makes it easy to be creative. With PageMaker, you can easily produce inexpensive, high-quality publications in a fraction of the time it takes using conventional methods.